PASSIVE INCOME

To John &
Maureen

Excellent

friends and

Clients

Nass

PASSIVE INCOME

How to give up your day job and put your feet up

ROSS PERRY

AuthorHouse™ UK Ltd.
1663 Liberty Drive
Bloomington, IN 47403 USA
www.authorhouse.co.uk
Phone: 0800.197.4150

Published by AuthorHouse 12/03/2013

ISBN: 978-1-4918-8730-1 (sc)
ISBN: 978-1-4918-8731-8 (e)

CONTENTS

INTRODUCTION AND BACKGROUND

For many years, I have worked in the financial services sector. First, I assisted banks, then worked with credit companies, and then I became an independent financial advisor. These experiences led me to realize of the power of passive income streams.

Passive income became a buzz idea around seven years prior to the writing of this book. I have read many books on the subject. None of them inspired me, but the subject always did. The majority of those books concentrated on narrow areas of the subject—particularly selling and advertising things online. Though I will discuss that specific topic, I hope to provide a more comprehensive guide that enables you to implement my ideas with your own ideas. I seek to achieve this goal by explaining the issue clearly.

Before I show you how to earn an attractive flow of money from multiple income streams, I need to set out some ground rules, a list of things that will keep you on the right path despite all the bumps in the road. By staying on this path, you can attain total financial security!

Why is it sensible to seek a path that deviates from more traditional forms of paid income? As recently as November of 2012, the Joseph Rowntree Organisation disclosed that, in the United Kingdom, six million workers were classified as poor. Note that the figure refers to *workers,* not people out of work. In fact, at the time of this writing, in-work poverty outstrips workless poverty (excluding pensioners).

1.4 million people are working part-time jobs despite wanting full-time work. That number has increased by 500,000 since 2009.

We have seen a real squeeze on the average person's wealth, accelerated by the banking crisis of 2008 and other factors. In fact, there are numerous causal links:

- Increasingly complex employment law alienates many employers and discourages them from increasing their workforce.
- Improved computer technology means fewer arms, legs, and brains are needed.
- Cheaper venues and labour exist abroad or in other countries within the eurozone.
- Continual inflation exceeds pay increases.

There are two other material factors relevant to this situation:

- A job for life is extremely rare these days.
- We are an ageing population.

I have read extensively about financial matters. I have considered the suggestion that financial diversification is a dirty word, but is it? If you are (or can become) an expert in a narrow field of skills that will be in demand, you will probably not be reading this. Even with those skills, you may suffer from a very sharp downturn of demand, subjecting your future income to high risks.

What is risk? Everything in life is a risk. It may be in your nature to avoid risks or embrace them. Your position in regards to risk could have arisen through your innate tolerances and thresholds, something positive or negative you experienced in your life, or a situation that is completely beyond your control.

As a financial advisor, I was asked frequently which areas people should invest in. The answer depends upon many factors, but investing in just one area increases your chance of catching a cold. Let us look at one area as an example. In recent times, buying property and letting it out was the ideal retirement solution for most people. Or so they thought. Before, during, and after the banking crisis, first-time buyers found it far more difficult to obtain a mortgage, and that was only one of the many indicators that the property lending market was retracting. For many first-time landlords, the party was coming to an end.

Many investors had built up considerable property portfolios by using a tool known as *gearing,* also called leverage. It is true that pure leverage is a powerful tool, but in some property markets, new and inexperienced landlords built up very high gearing ratios. Lenders allowed them to do this by injecting money into the market with easy loans given out at very competitive rates. High gearing represents a high level of borrowing in relation to your initial asset, usually your deposit. When the banking crisis hit, it was akin to a house of cards folding. If the whole of your financial position was invested in property, you might have experienced severe problems. This is not to say I am against buying and letting property—quite the opposite: such investments provide a valuable part of any exposure. But your investments should not be bound up in one area exclusively.

I could discuss other examples of being too exposed in certain asset classes, but I think the recent housing collapse is a suitable example. In short, you should embrace diversification.

WHAT IS PASSIVE INCOME?

Passive income is a system that requires initial research and guidance; but it's also a system that allows your money to work for you with little or no additional effort. Money carries on multiplying while you sleep, even though you are not contributing much effort.

Most people believe that the only way to earn money is to work for it. This model is known as linear income. Today, in at least 95 per cent of the Western world, this continues to be the case. Whatever your job, you have to get up, travel to work, and swap your own time for your weekly or monthly pay cheque. If you do not get up for work, your income stream will suffer or evaporate entirely.

As a financial advisor, most of my clients were people who had already retired or did not need to work. These clients are good examples of people who are beneficiaries of passive income. But pensioners with good income are not an exclusive club. You don't have to be old to be financially secure, but you do have to start as soon as you can. For all of you who work—even if you are one of the lucky few who enjoys doing a given job—imagine working because you *choose* to do so.

In the United Kingdom, as I write, the emergence of payday loans (loans with severe drawbacks) are constantly in the news for the wrong reasons. Yet, they remain popular. This is not a new phenomenon. There have been numerous criticisms about them in the press, but these complaints are only valid if the company in question is misleading its customers. After all, the company is carrying out a service that the customer agrees to because he or she is unable or unwilling to seek better terms elsewhere. The culmination of this situation is the explosion of outlets that buy gold. In these transactions who is the winner, the seller or the buyer? I think you already know the answer to that question.

Western stock markets typically function on a boom/bust dynamic. These periods of boom and bust are reasonably predictable. During a recession, workers' pay is frozen, rarely keeping pace with inflation. At the same time, simple things such as filling up your car, doing your weekly shopping, and paying your utility bills keeps getting harder. Payday loans work for the lender because they can charge fees for lending small amounts of money when a person is short that week, possibly because a massive electricity bill came in. There are also instances of high-paid executives who use payday loans to finance their lifestyles. Such a person is on a short rope!

Credit card companies love customers who pay the minimum balance on their credit cards (as long as they do not eventually default) because they make a fortune on the compounding debt. With the Bank of England interest rate at 0.5 per cent at the time of this writing, it does not take much to work out how much money banks and other lenders are earning when they charge 17 per cent or more. People who have average or poor credit ratings must pay considerably more in interest because they are forced into the sub-prime market to borrow money. Often, those people enter into a downward spiral that has no end unless they go into administration or bankruptcy. I know this is one extreme of the scale, but even if you are more fortunate than those facing bankruptcy, someone out there is making a fortune off of you and laughing all the way to the bank.

Who can you trust with your money? The short answer is *you.* You are responsible for your own decisions, but you should also have a team of advisors whom you can trust. This team might consist of people such as accountants, lawyers, and independent financial advisors.

There was a time that people had respect for institutions such as banks, but they have lost that respect. They are not decent financial role models anymore. It's a dog-eat-dog world, and if you get in the way, you are going to get bitten. It makes a mockery of regulation when the Financial Services Authority introduced legislation to treat customers fairly, but the banks continue lending too much, fixing LIBOR rates to their own ends, and selling PPI insurance improperly. Such practices on the part of the banks are largely invisible, and they have been going on for decades.

If you are an employee, whom can you trust with your job? Just yourself. There are very few jobs that a person can keep for life. You should be planning for the loss of your job on the first day you start that new job.

Is there an alternative to paid employment? Yes, but don't give up your day job until you are ready. Carefully plan on becoming financially secure from everything and everybody as soon as possible. I will demonstrate that, even if you start with little or nothing, you can start this process today and look forward to a point in your life when you are king.

The following people cannot benefit from the information in this book:

- People who are born with silver spoons in their mouths. Your bloodline is a lottery. Even those born into wealth often struggle to keep it.
- People who pick the six numbers for the National Lottery correctly. Unfortunately, the chance of doing this is one in nearly fourteen million. Even if you do win, your wealth and approach needs managing. History has shown that happiness spikes when you win the lottery, but that happiness often dissipates quickly. I am old enough to remember Vivien Nicholson. In 1961, she won over £152,000 (worth more than £3,000,000 in today's terms). When asked what she was going to do with the winnings, she said, 'Spend, spend, spend!' And she did exactly that. Not only did she spend her winnings quickly, she became affected emotionally.
- People who have spent a lifetime working in the linear income system. There is nothing wrong with this method. It is called earning a living, and most people only get this far.

As you might imagine, the line between linear and passive income can merge or become obscure. There are very few passive income sources that start off purely passive. In order to establish these sources, some linear effort is required (at least to start).

Often, I have heard people who run their own businesses claim that they are recipients of passive income. That is not true. If you are a company director, for example, who works every single day, you may be the business owner, but you will not join the private members' club unless you *sell* the business and live forever off the fat of the sale. Alternatively, you could get someone to run the business for you such that little or no effort is required of you. The second option is more difficult than it sounds: it is like someone else bringing up your baby.

Unless you want your company to survive past your life, you should start any new business with the end of it in mind. Have an exit strategy in place **from day one.**

Money is not everything. Wealth on its own does not make you happy. The best way to view wealth is to see how it provides options for you and your family. Think of the uncertainty and misery that is often associated with not having enough money. Now compare that state of living with being financially secure forever.

HOW MUCH MONEY IS ENOUGH?

It is difficult to quote a figure because we all have different views, needs, and wants. Additionally, any figure quoted will be subject to inflation and life expectancy. Inflation eats into money the same way certain chemicals rust metal. *Anything* you do with money carries a risk. Even hugely risk-averse people who do not look beyond simple bank deposits suffer from the risk inherent in interest rates. But realistically, how much is enough? If you put me on the spot, I'll say £1,000,000. One million smackers.

Throughout my professional and personal life, I have had access to sophisticated research that identified such things as funding and growth yields. In time, I deduced that a 5 per cent return was a good rule of thumb. That amount is not unrealistic if you are considering all your assets. To some, that number will seem low; to others, that number will seem a little too high. Nevertheless, it is not a bad figure.

With a million smackers yielding income at 5 per cent, you will have £50,000 per year, or £4167 per month before tax. Some of you will be thinking, *What about inflation?* Of course, you are 100 per cent correct: a million pounds 12 months later, would still be worth a million pounds *on paper,* but it would only buy you a million pounds less inflation. There is also the trivial matter of your tax liabilities, which I will cover later.

Without making the formula too complicated, you will need at least 1 million pounds + 5 per cent + the percentage of inflation over the previous year. The rate of return in the second year is dependent upon what happened the previous year. At this stage, we are not looking for capital appreciation (although that will be great if it happens), we are simply looking for a 5 per cent yield, which translates into income. And that income will grow sufficiently beyond the original amount to retain the true purchasing power of £1,000,000.

In year one, if we assume inflation is 3.2 per cent, you will need growth of around 8.94 per cent. That is, £50,000 to pay you the income and £32,000 to reflect the drag of inflation.

Here is the equation:

£1,000,000 - £82,000 = £918,000 + growth of 8.94% = £82,069.20 = £1,000,069.20

What I quoted, 5 per cent, is a nice figure, but 8.94 per cent is needed and will require a bit more of effort.

WHAT ABOUT DEBT?

You have probably heard about good debt and bad debt. *What madness!* you are probably thinking. *Surely, all debt is bad.* No, it is not. If people, companies, and governments stopped borrowing money, the civilized world would quickly grind to a halt. A true entrepreneur often uses other people's money through short-term loans to make money for himself or herself. Let's explore bad debt versus good debt.

Bad debt

John gets persuaded to take out a store card by a retail chain instead of writing out a cheque or using his debit card when he buys a washing machine. He pays 32 per cent APR on any outstanding balances existing on his statement at the end of the month. He buys more items in the store over the next six months and only pays the minimum balance by direct debit (as suggested by the salesman in the store). John very rarely looks at his bank statements, and he does not know what balancing his chequebook means. Very soon, his debt will spiral out of control because the debt is compounding.

Good debt

Maureen, an experienced investor and risk taker borrows £10,000 pounds from a bank over a full year. She pays a fixed interest rate of 6.2 per cent. She invests the bank's funds into an investment she feels has potential, and she is rewarded because the investment matures after a year, providing an after-tax return of 12.3 per cent. Therefore, the cost of borrowing is as follows: £10,000 + interest at 6.2 per cent = £10,620. She has serviced the debt from other income sources at a rate of £885 pounds per month. Her return is £11,230 minus £10,620, which equals £610 profit.

Lots of you reading this will be disturbed by Maureen's approach. Personally, I am far more disturbed by John's. Who is Maureen?

- An assertive risk taker.
- Someone who has done her research and feels confident that she will have a good return on her investment. There is no *guarantee* that she will, but her extensive research indicates that she likely will.
- Someone who has a diversified portfolio.
- Someone who does not follow the herd; she goes with what her own research indicates and what her gut tells her.
- Someone who self-funded the exercise from profits made on previous investments.
- Someone who benefitted from the practice of *compounding* and *leverage*.
- A passive income maker!

And who is John?

- A financially disinterested or uneducated person, but not someone who is stupid necessarily.

- Someone who considers himself savvy with the cash in his pocket.
- Someone who thinks saving is for the birds. He would rather spend his money as he earns it because he can't take it with him when he dies.
- Someone who does not really know what an APR is.

All lenders love disinterested customers because they rarely ask questions. As long as the customer pays all the debt back with the combined interest, the lender is happy.

We are all very different people, so what makes us tick? Maslow's theory is a good example of how we tick. In his paper, a theory of human motivation, Maslow argued that there are five stages to human fulfilment.

Stage 1

The first requirement for humans is our physiological needs. In order to survive, we need the basics: food, shelter, air, and water. Without these, we would not be around for long!

Stage 2

The second requirement is safety and security. We need financial security, and fear of losing our jobs is always in the back of our minds. For those of you who have suffered such an ordeal at one time or another, you know that it feels like your life has caved in.

Stage 3

The third requirement is love and belonging. In order to function well, all of us need to feel that we have friends, a family, and someone with whom we can be intimate. This, to some extent, can occur outside of family units. Some examples include football teams, gangs, and clubs.

Stage 4

The fourth requirement is esteem. We all need to feel respected; we all seek recognition. While discussing recognition, an old colleague of mine once said, 'Babies cry for it; soldiers die for it.' The words are a bit extreme, but you get the point.

Stage 5

The fifth requirement is self-actualization. In a nutshell, we want to be all that we can be. This is achieved when we accomplish something very important.

There are some critics of Maslow's theory, but I believe it to be valid. What concerns me are modern-day attitudes about employment. Even if you have reached the top of the ladder, everything can come crashing down if you lose your job. You will be shot back to level one, human survival. Or is it even worse than that? How many of us have read about parents in the United Kingdom skimping on food in order to afford the bus fare to send their kids to school or keep the heat on? Currently, many people have contempt for benefit recipients, yet there are thousands of people who are entitled to benefits but do not claim them.

Generally, unless you know what you are doing with debt—and you control it—it is sensible not to have any debt.

Using my simple scenario of £1,000,000 at 5 per cent gives you £4,167pcm *without* the need to service debt. That is a great base.

Breaking debt down even further, we must examine debt that you pay because you have no choice and debt that you pay voluntarily. Naturally, for our purposes, I am only interested in the latter category.

Examples of mandatory debt:

- mortgage or rent
- utility bill
- council tax
- telephone bill
- food
- travel expenses
- certain education expenses

Examples of voluntary debt; that is disposable income.

- buying a case of fine wine
- trips to the cinema or the theatre
- taking your loved ones out to a fancy restaurant
- buying a season ticket for your footie team.

- a cruise around the Med.
- giving to your favourite charity

There is one element I have not mentioned yet: time. You need time on your side for all of the following reasons:

- The older you are, the less time you have left to live.
- The older you are, the more difficult the linear approach becomes due to the physical and mental stress of ageing. In a nutshell, it becomes harder to do your job.
- Becoming proficient at building multiple passive income streams means you need time to research.
- You need time to think and plan.
- You need time to evaluate and change your plan based upon what is working.
- You need time to learn from your mistakes (yes, you will make them).
- You need time to let compounding work its magic.

By now, you have picked up on the fact that I have mentioned compounding a couple of times. But what is it? I like to think of it this way: the bigger the numbers, the easier they grow. The simple weight of money grows exponentially if you are doing it right and have it in the right places. Furthermore, anyone who says using one investment idea or vehicle as opposed to another is better is either lying, inexperienced, or lucky. History proves that a *balanced asset* category approach is often the most successful. In simple terms, if one of your ideas fall flat or underperforms, your other assets can often pick up the slack.

Compounding, in its basic form, entails interest being added to the capital. Later, more interest is added to the increased capital. However, to receive passive income, you will need far more than interest being added to capital. In a very low interest rate environment, you will receive more value by spending your money now rather than letting inflation erode your wealth. As mentioned before, you need at least 5 per cent plus the rate of inflation, year on year, to keep your 5 per cent per annum income intact.

One asset you will need is the right attitude. You have to believe that, even if you are only starting with £10, the day will come when you have £1,000,000.

In summary, to benefit from passive income, you need:

- the right attitude
- time to research
- time for your plan to mature

Start by building up a portfolio of ideas. My ideas include the following:

- Make a plan and record what your initial resources are. What assets you are going to have in your portfolio?
- Keep an updated record of what your income and expenses are. Also record your assets and liabilities. This is easily achieved on an Excel spreadsheet.
- Don't give up your day job whilst you are building your asset base. One day you can choose to quit.

PASSIVE INCOME STREAMS

Idea 1: Form your own business that you can sell eventually.

Why should you run your own business? There are many reasons:

Control

Being the boss of your own company means that you control more or less everything that goes on. You do not have a superior who can walk into your office and say that you are no longer required. This happened to me only once in my career, when I worked for an American bank. At the time, I felt like the world had ended. My boss walked in, gave me my marching orders, and told me to leave without speaking to any of my staff. He did this two weeks before Christmas, and I had a young family. How anyone could do that, I have no idea. Unfortunately for them, they underestimated me. A few weeks later, they had to pay me some meaningful compensation. It taught me a good lesson, however: prepare for the worst and avoid giving others such authority.

You might be thinking, *Okay, but what should I do?*

Have an idea and keep it simple.

Stick to things you know. It might be a hobby; it might be something you have been trained to do. Make sure you like what you do. There is nothing more unpleasant than hating the work you do and the people you work with. Being miserable will affect your performance and cut the soul out of you. Do not deviate materially from what you are trying to succeed at. You will only take your eye off the ball. This is something else that I have done in the past, and it is a waste of time and money.

Have a business that is saleable.

Your business must have value. You must profit from it; otherwise, it will not qualify as passive income. If you need to go to work every day to make it work, it falls under the heading of linear income. You will likely be linear for some time, but the goal is to become a passive income maker. You can work on other passive ideas at the same time. This is what I did. Do not lose sight of the intention to start a business that you can sell one day.

Have a plan.

Someone once said, 'If you fail to plan, plan to fail.' This is one saying that should be on every person's wall. You must have targets. Many of you know the SMART principle. If you do not know it, here it is:

S stands for *specific.*

M stands for *measureable.*

A stands for *achievable.*

R stands for *realistic.*

T stands for *time-bound* (you must know when everything is going to happen).

As John 'Hannibal' Smith from the legendary and fictional A-Team often said, 'I love it when a plan comes together.' He was not wrong.

Tax

The clever financial author, Robert T Kiyosaki, provides wonderful insights in his *Rich Dad, Poor Dad* books. One aspect of running your own business is controlling and creating your own turnover and profits. You also have some control over how much tax you pay. You can buy legitimate items for your business that become gross deductions from expenditures. Most people buy items after tax from our net pay.

Take a simple example: a laptop computer. Recently, I bought a nice Toshiba laptop. Let's say it cost £500. This £500 expense is deducted from my gross turnover. At the time of this writing, the United Kingdom tax authorities still treat new computers as 100 per cent deductible, and that £500 counts against any corporation tax that my company must pay.

Arnold, who is a 40 per cent UK tax payer, is a non-controlling employee of a company; therefore, he bought his computer *after* he paid 40 per cent tax on his income. Thus, it actually cost him £835 in real terms.

With my company, I sold most of the assets of my business by transferring clients and a repetitive income stream that I now receive a return on each month. It took me twenty years to build up this passive income steam. My company now receives a good percentage of most funds under management in various investments. The turnover for this source may dissipate over time. After all, when my company was active, we suffered 100 per cent of the costs, but now we pay a tiny fraction of that amount. In addition to the obvious costs such as training, travel, and salary, we also avoid regulatory fees. I am no longer directly responsible for the compliance of that sector of the business. Most importantly, I no longer have to turn up to work every day. The parent company that purchased mine is also benefiting from passive income. In some cases, the staff must administer and advise the client bank in a linear fashion.

In summary, what are you good at? What do you enjoy doing? Is this something that can create turnover and profit for you? Who is your target market? How are you going to sell and market your product or service? What are the potential expenses? Will a bank lend to you?

At the end of this process, once successful, you will need to sell it to benefit passively. Do not hold on to your baby. Like in real life, you have to let them go when they are grown.

Banks, despite their recent bad press, like to lend to entrepreneurs. You may need staff to help you run your business, especially if you wish to spend more time working *on* your business rather than *in* it. Hiring staff these days is potentially problematic and expensive. To get the best out of your staff, you need to treat them fairly. If you don't do this, you could be heading to an industrial tribunal, which could spell your ruin.

You need to understand the difference between a business owner and an employee. At first, this may be hard for you because you've never been an owner. Think about what you thought of your employer, and then imagine how your employees see you. Chances are, as an employee, you thought one or more of the following things:

- My employer is not paying me anywhere near what I am worth.
- My co-workers seem to get better perks.
- My boss does not realize that, when he goes on holiday, I am the one who is generating the profits to keep the business going.
- The company should increase my pay, pension, and other benefits. After all, what they are paying me is a bit insulting.
- Why do they keep increasing my targets?
- That last venue the company took us to for a Christmas lunch was insulting. They could have afforded to take us to a first-class establishment.

Whichever Western democracy you live in, you cannot pick up a newspaper or see the six o'clock news without hearing about one firm or another making staff redundant or facing staffing issues. If you are a member of a company doing something along those lines, you might well believe that you are much more valuable than your controlling boss. You have to accept, however, that the main difference between you and your boss is that he takes *100 per cent* of the risk; you take none. You might start at 9:00 a.m. and finish at 5:00 p.m. with an hour off for lunch. You might never notice that your boss is in the office on Saturday or Sunday.

As a business owner, you take 100 per cent of the risk. It is only fair, then, that you are entitled to most of the reward. I wonder how many business owners actually take most of the reward . . . I suspect only a small percentage.

Also, try to think about your employer's perspective of you. Taking out all the niceties and personalities, your employer thinks of you as a financial unit. As a financial unit, are you a profit or a cost centre for the business? If you are a profit centre, how much profit are you making? If you are a cost centre, how long will the organisation retain your services before you are history?

If you are not prepared to take 100 per cent of the risk, you should probably remain an employee. Don't chastise yourself if you do that; after all, you are in the majority. There are still many things you can do to benefit from passive income streams, but you will *never* benefit unless you are prepared to take on at least some risk.

Once you are prepared to take risk, have a plan, and want to start a business, you may wish to speak to a bank manager. He or she will want to see the following:

- A sensible and logical business plan.
- A cash flow projection.
- Some security. This may include tangible and personal guarantees. If you are not prepared to put up equity for a stake in the business, why should a bank lend to you and take all the risk?
- The bank manager will want to interview you to get an idea of your motivation.
- The bank will want to know when it will get its money back. This will give it confidence to lend you more in the future when you will be in a stronger position to negotiate rates.
- Banks are not the only source of money, but they are the most common. Venture capital organisations are available, but they will likely want a higher return and some shares in your company.
- At some point in the future, you could become self-funding. You could become your own bank.

Idea 2: Explore crowdfunding.

Zopa

These next few ideas come from the direct financial services sector. What else would you expect from a financial advisor?

I came across Zopa about three years ago, when I was doing some other research. I saw the concept straight away. Zopa is a company that enables the public to lend and borrow from each other directly, thus cutting out the middleman: the bank.

As a lender this is how it works: Cynthia wants to borrow £8,000 to buy a car. Her bank is either unwilling to lend her the full amount or has offered her an uncompetitive rate. She turns to Zopa after finding them on a price comparison website. After credit vetting her, they agree to lend her the full amount.

Where do they get the funds from? They turn to lenders like me. However, I do not take the full risk of lending her the £8,000. I only lend her, say, £10. Thus, for Cynthia to get her full loan, she needs the participation of eight hundred lenders, each of whom pays £10. This *dramatically* reduces my exposure as a lender, but I still have a say in how much interest I will charge on the capital. The higher the interest I want to charge, the lower the take up of my capital. If Cynthia does not like the rate, she can refuse to borrow my £10; if she likes it, she would. Zopa is the facilitator. It brings Lenders and borrowers together, for a fee to both.

Zopa pools the funds from various different lenders whom she has approved. After that, a deal is struck.

Zopa also conducts the credit checking and handles the administration tasks. The business owners and shareholders of Zopa have come up with a brilliant concept, and they benefit from passive income streams. In my view, everybody wins.

From the lender's perspective:

- You set how much your exposure is. It might be £10 as a minimum, but you could increase the exposure if you wanted to.
- Ten pounds is a small risk.
- You set the interest rate and Zopa gives you an indication of whether it is competitive.
- Zopa does the credit vetting.
- Zopa manages the geography and brings the buyer and seller together. If I live in London and Cynthia lives in Birmingham, Cynthia would not likely travel to London to borrow the funds.
- Zopa has bonded bank accounts, which means that, if they fail, the money can be retrieved from a third-party company.
- You benefit from compounding. If you do not constantly demand funds from Zopa, the interest payments you receive from them get *rolled together* with any new capital you introduce. Over time, when the numbers get bigger, compounding has a very beneficial effect.
- The risk is small, not only because you are lending a small amount, but also because there is no equity risk. This is in contrast to a managed share portfolio, where share prices can fall or rise in capital value. With Zopa, interest is payable, so you should receive a steady return.
- It is not likely that you will encounter bad debt, but even if you do, the written-off amount is small by comparison.
- You get to choose the markets you invest in. You can lend to anyone who has passed Zopa's credit

checks. You might decide to lend only to category A clients. If you do, your risk factor will be lower, but your return will be lower, too.

- If for any reason you want the majority of your capital back quickly, Zopa will offer to redistribute your loans to other Zopa lenders (for an additional fee, of course).
- Zopa recently introduced a new safeguard fund that, for a lower return, removes any chance of bad debt by underwriting it (for a fee, of course).

From the borrower's perspective:

- You have the opportunity to borrow the funds at a more competitive rate than what your bank or sub-prime lender offered you.
- No heavies at your door demanding weekly or monthly repayments. All repayments are transacted by direct debit.
- No lengthy interview processes.
- Quick and easy fund turnarounds, meaning you do not lose your dream car.

From Zopa's perspective:

- No capital risk. They simply put borrowers in touch with lenders.
- They can charge the borrower a fee.
- They can charge the lender a fee.
- They can charge the lender an additional fee if the lender wants the capital back quickly.

Everybody wins? I think so.

When you stop funding capital and receive a passive return, you redirect returns—both capital and interest—into a holding account and have the funds paid back into your account. This qualifies this process as passive income. This is another source of income that can be coupled with your other processes to give you the desired bottom line when the time is right.

Potential disadvantages to Zopa:

- You can only receive most of your funds back quickly by paying an additional fee.
- All institutions can fail. If Zopa fails, it is unlikely to be bailed out by the government
- Zopa is not protected by the financial ombudsman service, but it will be soon (the company has applied to become regulated under the Financial Conduct Authority).
- Tax is payable on interest you receive.

I have set up accounts both personally and through a company with Zopa. There are advantages and disadvantages to using these mediums.

Advantages to personal account:

These are personal funds and do not form part of the company balance sheet.

Disadvantages to personal account:

You have to pay personal tax up to the highest rate of tax to start the capital. You are liable for further tax and fees on future interest payments.

Advantages to company account:

You can control (to a certain extent) how much tax you will pay on future returns, particularly if you introduce the initial capital to Zopa via the company as a director's loan. If tax is payable on returns at the small business rate, this is payable at 20 per cent at the time of writing, not the 40 per cent rate for personal tax.

Disadvantages to company account:

It is a company asset, not yours directly. It will be harder to get your hands on it, at least to some extent. It is entered on the company balance sheet. If the company is making good profits, it will have to pay proportionate taxes.

Funding Circle

This company is similar to Zopa. The difference is that the investor lends to a commercial enterprise rather than an individual. Again, the risk is dissipated because, as an investor, you can lend as little as £10 to each and every business. The businesses are credit vetted as before, but because you are lending to a business, the returns and risks are likely to be higher.

Crowdcube

This is a variation of Funding Circle. With this model, you lend to start-up businesses. You have the potential to take an equity stake in the business, and your loans are likely to benefit from tax relief through the Enterprise Investment Schemes (EIS).

Crowdcube is also regulated by the Financial Conduct Authority, which offers additional security to the investor and access to the Financial Ombudsman Service (FOS), which covers investors if they feel they have been misled.

General points, inflation, and the power of compounding and pound cost averaging

At this point it is appropriate go off on a tangent and continue discussing compounding. We need to review pound cost averaging. This principle works for a lot of your assets, not just interest-bearing accounts.

In its simplest form, compounding is a simple concept. As previously mentioned, it is interest added to capital, attracting higher value returns. Over time the weight of your asset can grow exponentially.

For example, if you save £150 every month over twenty-five years and receive a constant 5 per cent interest, you will receive a return of £88,218. This is what all simple calculations will tell you, but that is not the end of the story. Remember our enemy *inflation?*

You may have over £88,000 pounds in your pocket, but there is no way it will have the same value it did twenty-five years ago. You can continue the same argument in favour of inflation with the monthly funding scenario because, over the three hundred months you paid your £150, the same amount would come out of your bank account every month. Gradually and over time, it would not actually cost you £150, it would cost you *less*. This is because both the monthly contribution you make *and* the capital value are being eroded by inflation.

Pound cost averaging

This is the same concept and can be best approached using unit trust-style equity investments instead of just cash. Here, the value of your assets and value of the individual shares change on a daily basis because they can both fall and rise in value. The only item that is averaged is the amount you put in on a monthly basis.

A simple example is as follows: Joan puts £50 a month into a stock. In month one, her £50 buys 23.27 units of the managed fund she is in. In month two, the same amount buys 21.95 units (1.32 less than month one). In month three, the same amount buys 29.55 (6.28 more than month one). Over three months, Joan has accumulated 74.77 units in the stock at a price of £150. She has averaged 24.92 units. This demonstrates that it is profitable to invest in a falling market that later recovers.

What do a lot of people do? Most of us suffer from the herd instinct. We sell when a market is falling and buy when a market is rising. Panic is a horrible emotion. Selling a stock when it is falling is okay if you decided to do that from outset. *Stop loss* is a term that may be familiar to a some of you. This is a price you force yourself to sell at to stem potential future losses. Of course, you could be wrong: the price may well recover.

When I first started advising, it was common to see younger people saving regularly. Nowadays, it is less common. This reality will likely be a big problem for a lot of younger savers (unless they have rich relatives or partners). As of the time of this writing, mortality rates are as follows: a male baby is expected to live 78.1 years and a female is expected to live 82.1 years.* That is the highest age we have ever seen, and as medical science advances, new generations will live even longer. The biblical phrase outlining a typical life—'three score years and ten'—should now be written as follows: 'Almost four score!'

My father was born in 1912 and died in 1983 (not quite seventy-one). He retired at sixty; most of his peers retired at sixty-five. He was a senior bank executive, so as you might expect, he knew how to save and appreciated the value of money. He was also a member of an occupational pension scheme that provided guaranteed benefits. For all sorts of reasons, these schemes are going through their death throes.

Occupational schemes offer *guaranteed* benefits based on the average of your highest salary over the number of years of your employment. It was then divided by a common accrual rate, typically sixty.

So an employee who worked forty years (usually the maximum), whose last year's salary (or an average of the best three years in the previous ten years) of £25,000 would receive £16,667 pounds in the first year of retirement, and the number would automatically increase each year to help with the cost of inflation. Furthermore, some of the pension fund could be commuted to pay a pension commencement lump sum, which is tax free. Furthermore, if you were married, the scheme provided a widow/widower pension as well.

My father was one of the lucky ones of his generation because he received a full bank pension at sixty rather than sixty-five. At sixty-five he started drawing his state pension and obtained income from his savings as well. If he had retired at the normal pension age of sixty-five, and if his pension escalated at 3 per cent per annum, he would have received the following:

- age 66: £16667
- age 67: £17167
- age 68: £17682
- age 69: £18212
- age 70: £9379 (half a year because of death)

A total of £79,107 plus state pension . . . guaranteed.

- *Source Office of National statistics

  Today, people are retiring earlier, changing occupations more frequently (both voluntarily and involuntarily), and living longer. The problem is, you cannot compare on an exact like-for-like basis because the model in the eighties cannot compare to what is happening today.

- People are living much longer, and unless there is a global catastrophe in the future, that trend will escalate. Ladies, you will notice that you have the bigger problem because, on average, you live four years longer than men (although the gap is slowly narrowing, apparently).

- Occupational pension schemes are fizzling out, and not just because of our increased longevity. They are disappearing *fast*. I often sympathize with employer vs. employee conflicts over pay and pensions, but to a large extent, you cannot believe the employer is at fault (unless the employer is Robert Maxwell). Most occupational schemes are unsustainable.

- The alternative to an occupational pension scheme is a money purchase scheme. This is where the staff member takes the risk on fund performance, and to some extent, the costs of the scheme. This time there are no guarantees concerning the starting pension.

- As a nation, we are not saving anywhere near the amount we need to.

- Annuity rates are dropping and will continue to drop. An annuity entails swapping a pension fund for an insurance company to agree to pay you a certain amount of money for the rest of your life. Most people my age remember annuity rates being 10 per cent or 10p income for every £1 swapped. Nowadays, a lot of people receive half of that.

- In past generations, people worked for one employer for a long time. Those days have long gone. Part-time workers are exceptionally common.

Most people who work part-time jobs don't do it by choice; they would prefer full-time employment.

Why is this relevant? Simply, if a lot of you do not wake up and smell the coffee, it will be too late. You could be looking at working not because you chose to, but because you have to.

Here is another fact: most people twenty-five or under are more capable of dealing with the mental and physical demands of linear income (working, swapping time for money). When you are sixty-five (at a time when people are expected to work and live longer), do you think doing the same job will be easier or harder? You already know the answer. There are exceptions to the rule. A lot of people over sixty-five like to work at B&Q, for example.

Idea 3: Become a landlord and rent properties.

If you read the same financial books that I do, you'll learn that a lot of self-made millionaires made their wealth exclusively from property. These schemes are still at the heart of the passive income success stratagem, but you must do some research to try to understand what you are doing.

About ten years ago, there was a frenzy of do-it-yourself, amateur landlords with the opinion that buying a property, doing it up, and selling it on (or buying it and renting it out) was the only way to build up a substantial and supportive passive income stream. For many landlords, I am sure that was the case. But in my experience, following a limited investment philosophy can get you into trouble because, with a narrow investment horizon, you increase the level of risk you take. In the last recession, inexperienced investor landlords started getting very uncomfortable about their debt vs. equity exposure (often referred to as *gearing*).

Like any other passive income sources, rentals have their advantages and disadvantages. However, as part of a *balanced portfolio,* property can be an essential component.

What is the target market?

- domestic and commercial purchases, refurbishment, and selling for a profit
- domestic and commercial purchases, refurbishment, and rental
- holiday lets
- student lets

Domestic purchases are the most common purchases.

Buying with the view of refurbishment and selling on

If you intend to buy a rundown property, do it up, and sell it, it's best to ensure that you do not own a property already. Otherwise, you might have to pay capital gains tax if you are buying and selling as an individual, and you at least need to be living in that property for some time prior to be classified as it's homeowner

At the time of writing, it is still very much a buyers' market, so rentals benefit more than purchases and resales. Of course, financial cycles being financial cycles, this situation may well revert. But if you intend to buy a property to resell it later on, you need to consider various things:

- What is your budget?
- Who is going to do the refurbishment, you or someone else? If you are doing it yourself, you should factor in your own worth on a cost-per-hour basis. If you are not doing it, you will most likely be earning money somewhere else. In any event, this is still a linear model. At least initially.
- What is your time frame? Remember the *SMART* principle.
- How long can you keep the property before you *must* sell it?
- What is the location of the property, and does it make economic sense?
- If you are buying the property at an auction, have an upper limit on your spending. Do not get caught in the moment—a lot of people do.
- If you are buying from an estate agent, what commission rate can you negotiate? If you intend to buy to rent the property, the same agent may be tempted to reduce commission if he or she can act as a landlord agent in the future.
- Do you need to get a mortgage for the purchase, and if so, will the lender let you redeem the mortgage in three months, six months, or a year?
- A good approach is to consider future remortgages, which inject you with future *tax-free* capital.
- Stick to your budget. The majority of people go over it, which is understandable (especially if they are not experienced in the field).

- Remember: you are not buying the house for you. Buyers often want to stamp their own preferences on properties, which is why they go over budget. Your taste will very rarely match someone else's.
- When decorating the house, stick to neutral colours and contours. This means your prospective buyer will have the option of changing the design or keeping it as he or she sees fit.

It is important to appoint excellent professional advisors. Once you do, build up a consistent connection with them. Yes, this will come at a cost, but you can factor the cost in. And unless you are a qualified accountant, solicitor, or financial advisor, you may be shooting in the dark. The best way to find one is still the word-of-mouth method. If a friend or professional contact you have known for some time explains that he or she has had a good experience with his or her advisors, you would be silly not to heed that advice.

Our solicitors in Spain and England have saved me a fortune, as have our accountants in England.

Buying with a view to rent

I have bought property commercially and domestically for rental purposes. These properties have formed good investment vehicles for my passive income portfolio. I have had the most success renting apartments.

These are the advantages:

- You can usually get flexible mortgages that you do not need to redeem quickly.
- The theory, and often the practice, is that the tenant indirectly picks up all your costs when he or she pays you rent.
- Refurbishment, repairs, furnishing, and most other costs are tax deductible.
- Your property will increase in value over time. This means that you can remortgage later and take the tax-free proceeds.
- You should receive regular, monthly rent. Any positive balance after the mortgage payments and other costs is passive income.

Do not worry if your costs and expenses exceed your rental asset at first. Capital losses, unlike gains, can be carried forward, and they can be useful on balance with your other sources of income. Over time, unless you are extremely unfortunate, the value of the property will rise against your mortgage, the latter of which should remain static on an interest-only basis.

Location is an important aspect. Buying a property in Leeds or Birmingham will be cheaper than buying it in SE, SW, or central London. The borough of Westminster is the most expensive area in the United Kingdom to buy, but it will offer you the greatest rent potential. You need to work out a ratio of costs vs. income. I found, for example, that rental incomes in apartments in the Midlands were similar to rental incomes in Kent, but the purchase price was considerably cheaper in the Midlands. This is a good example of the quality of research.

Get yourself a good rental agent. You might pay up to 10 per cent of the rental fees, but the agent should do everything for you. It is like that person is the landlord. If you try to do it yourself, you may come unstuck. And even if you can pull it off, you are engaging in linear activity, not passive.

Make sure you obtain insurance against tenants who may default. This could cover a lot of contingent liabilities, though probably not all of them. Make sure you buy landlord insurance for the property.

Potential disadvantages to personal buy to lets:

- What category of tenant are you going to seek? DSS-style tenants are the highest risk, particularly now that local councils pay rent to the tenant directly in most cases.
- There are no guarantees that tenants will always pay. But if you have a mortgage, you still have to pay it.
- Costs can mount up, particularly with annual health and safety checks and other costs (such as boiler maintenance and other contracts).
- If you do not get a good property agent, he or she could be on the phone with every single problem that presents itself. We are back to linear activity again.

Idea 4: Gain returns from financial investments.

With this section, you either have capital to invest or you don't. If you don't, it would be sensible to allocate some regular savings to compounding and pound/cost averaging schemes.

Individual Savings Accounts (ISAs)

Commonly, there are two types of ISAs, cash and Maxi ISAs. Limits apply to what you can invest in each year. The limits generally rise each year.

In my view, at a time when interest rates for savers is the lowest it has been for a generation, cash ISAs should only be used if you are going to park the funds there for a very short time (e.g., for a deposit on a property).

With Maxi ISAs, you can invest conventionally or via the self-select method.

Conventional

These are typically known as collectives, such as unit trusts and/or open-ended funds.

I favour a 'supermarket' approach. This is where your financial advisor, on your behalf, goes to one provider who will have private funds and access to many external funds as well. The ISA allowance is per individual, and as mentioned, the limits typically increase each year. There is no limit on ISA transfers. If you are trying to build up capital, you are doing it as a lump sum, a monthly investment, or both. The fund approach is likely to be more adventurous than the income fund approach because you are not at the stage yet when you are receiving passive income. Which funds you will go into will be subject to your own circumstances and risk profile. Your professional advisor should be independent.

Whenever possible, try to subscribe to the full annual allowance. You do not have to fund it in one go, you will have an entire tax year to do just that.

When the time is right to receive passive income from this source, it is a good idea to flip the funds over to high-yielding income funds that pay out dividends. Through your provider, you can elect to receive income on a monthly basis or when the dividends are declared and paid. Do the latter. That way, you avoid surrendering part of your capital so the provider can pay the income.

Though there is a small amount of tax levied inside ISA funds, capital and dividend income received are tax free.

Your financial advisor will want to time when you switch funds designed for capital appreciation to income funds. He or she will not want to do this when markets are low, just in case you crystallize a loss on the investment. Sometimes, I found it hard to convince clients that they only crystallize a gain or a loss on investment when they move it around by switching it or taking it. While it is invested, even though unit prices may be depressed when the markets are down, you still have the same or an increased number of underlying units that can rise in value later on. So do not concern yourself with this matter. Do not follow the herd and panic sell.

The best scenario when you are taking income from ISA income funds is to achieve growth on your capital as well. This is a bonus, and it will help your battle against inflation.

Of course, if you have a partner, your funding allowances are doubled. Each tax year is a new ISA subscription, and even if you do not have new funds to inject, you can invest from other holdings you have such as unit trusts outside of an ISA tax wrapper. Be careful, though: do not surrender units if this makes you liable for capital gains tax, or if there are any inherent penalties in the action. There has to be a very good reason to surrender any current investments that leads crystallization of loss on capital.

An ISA-to-ISA switch, where appropriate, can be achieved without incurring any potential tax liabilities because it is achieved from provider to provider internally. They used to call this exercise *bed and breakfasting*.

Always consult an IFA

- IFAs usually suggest that you review your portfolio on a regular basis. Even if it is a cost to you, you should do it. The law requires you to have an MOT on cars that are not new once per year to ensure the cars are still roadworthy. Surely, even though there is no law saying that you have to review your financial situation on a regular basis, it makes sense to do it. Call me overindulgent if you wish, but I review my whole portfolio on a *daily* basis. If you want to be a true recipient of passive income, you will do the same.

- It is impossible for all companies and product providers to be great at everything. Of course, many claim that they are. It is highly unlikely that the provider you buy your ISA from is also a top pension or investment provider.

Self-select ISAs

Typically, you go online, choose a provider, and buy individual shares from approved ISA markets. On the surface, this might be a cheaper option, but it is subject to more risk because you select a narrower range of stocks in the form of direct company shares. Of course, you can do this on an execution-only basis. If you ask a firm to give you advice on this activity, it can become quite expensive. In the unit trust collective alternative, various fund managers will have invested in a whole basket of shares held within one fund. The more experienced you become, the more you should invest in both types.

Investment bonds

A very good source of potential passive income (especially, for those who do not need the capital back quickly) is an investment bond.

You can invest in them in the following ways:

- onshore
- offshore
- conventionally
- through pension funds

The best aspect of this product at present is the ability to receive 5 per cent of the original capital each year without any immediate liability to personal tax. This is a tax-deferred arrangement. If you received 5 per cent of capital each year, it would take twenty years for you to become liable for any tax.

The 5 per cent payments feel like income to you, but they are not. They are partial surrenders of your capital, with any growth designed to replenish your withdrawals. However, there is no guarantee they will unless you go into products that promise this from the outset. Like most financial products, the greater the risk, the greater the reward, the greater the chance of loss.

You have a whole range of product providers and funds that you can invest in.

Advantages to onshore bonds.

- A full 5 per cent of capital being paid has a tax-deferred status.
- It can be written on a life-assured basis or a capital-redemption basis. With the first scenario, the bond must end if the policyholder dies. With

the second scenario, the bond must end when the beneficiaries say so.

- You can receive payments for up to twenty years without the need to pay tax.

- Basic-rate tax is already deducted directly from onshore bonds. If you surrender all or more than the 5 per cent entitlement—as long as you are a basic-rate tax payer when you surrender the balance—there is no more tax to pay.

- If you were a higher-rate tax payer when you took out the bond and became a basic rate one before you surrendered it, onshore bonds can be a huge plus factor.

Advantages to offshore bonds

- They benefit in one crucial way, but they can bite you later. If they are invested with a traditional provider (in Dublin or the Isle of Man, say), the bond benefits from *gross roll up*. This means that the underlying funds, unlike onshore bonds, cannot be taxed directly by the UK government, nor will you pay immediate tax as long as no more than 5 per cent of the capital investment per annum is taken. However, you could be liable for 40 per cent tax when the bonds are surrendered. This makes them harder to surrender if you want to move the capital somewhere else.

Any type of bond should be considered a long-term investment. Therefore, try to devise your passive income portfolio to reflect the time element. The shorter the period of time, the more defensive the outlook (with cash at the head of the portfolio). This idea affects your immediate income requirements. Investment bonds (as well as some other products) should be toward the back of your portfolio.

Individual company shares are very easy to buy, and you can build up a portfolio online. There is an awful lot of data available to you about what to buy, when to buy it, and where to buy it. Equally, there are hundreds of theories about which approach is best. For the purposes of this book, however, passive income is achieved in the following ways:

- receiving dividends from the shares
- buying and selling shares for profit

In both cases, be careful about any tax liabilities. Get advice where appropriate.

There is a lot of information about spread betting. I am not going to dwell on this matter here, though, because spread betting is just gambling.

Idea 5: Taking effective Passive income from your pension funds.

Depending on your age, pensions will benefit you in the short term or the long term. If it is short term, I hope you have established mature pension funds already. The essential element to successful pension funding is timing. The earlier you start, the better.

These days, most pension funds, unless they are occupational schemes, can be accessed from age fifty-five onwards. There are many ways to invest:

- Invest directly with an insurance company. These funds are known as insured funds.
- Invest via a self-invested personal pension (SIPP). You can invest via insurance companies or you can get a SIPP directly from a SIPP operator.
- You can get a commercial arrangement through your own company. This is known as a Small Self-Administered fund (SSAS)
- You can have a family trust arrangement.

With any pension product, you should get advice. I will review the main differences shortly. However, let us look at the basic reasons why any passive income strategy should include pensions:

- Non tax payers can receive tax relief on pension contributions subject to a maximum annual investment of £3,600 gross. This only costs £2,880 net because you receive basic tax relief of £720 from HMRC.
- Basic tax payers can invest 100 per cent of their taxable pay. If you earn £30,000, you can make a contribution of £30,000. And if you did that, it would only cost you £24,000 because of the tax relief attracted by paying the contribution personally.
- Higher-rate tax payers get more tax relief, to their highest rate of tax.

When you take benefits from any age past 55, most pension schemes will allow you to receive a minimum of 25 per cent tax-free cash, known as a *pension commencement lump sum*. Later on, if you receive this in regular instalments from phased pension drawdown arrangements, it can become one of the jewels in your portfolio and passive income crown.

What is the main difference between self-investment and the alternative? The choice of assets you can invest in. Self-investment not only allows you to invest in pension funds, but also to invest in (amongst other things):

- unit trusts/OEICS(Open ended funds)
- individual shares in quoted and unquoted companies
- bank accounts
- investment bonds
- complex investments such as derivatives, and
- commercial property.

Before we go any further, let us imagine you have accumulated three different investment classes. To keep the maths simple, we will say you have £100,000 in an investment bond; £100,000 accumulated in a unit trust individual savings account; and £100,000 in a personal pension fund. Taking into account my rule of thumb (that you want to receive a 5 per cent yield), you would receive the following in one year:

- £5,000 from the investment bond
- £3,900 from the ISA
- £5,000 from the pension

That is a total of £13,900, and there is no need to pay tax immediately. How has this been achieved?

Investment bond

The 5 per cent in this case is not an assumptive figure. If you take more than 5 per cent of the original capital in one year, you are likely to trigger a tax charge. If you receive between 0 per cent and 5 per cent, you have no immediate liability to tax. Furthermore, if you do not need to take your 5 per cent in any given tax year, you do not lose the accumulation.(depending whether or not your IFA picks the right Product Provider) So with your £100,000 investment, if you deferred receiving capital for four years, you would be allowed to receive £100,000 x 5 per cent x 4 = £20,000. And there is no immediate liability to tax. Take into account that the formula is based on *the capital amount invested,* not the actual fund value or time of receipt. Thus, after four years, if your fund value rose £112,000 (or even if it lost £10,000 worth of value), you'd still receive the 5 per cent on £100,000. That is, you'd receive the original capital invested.

The ISA via a unit trust portfolio

Typically, if you are receiving income, all or part of your funds will be invested in high-yielding income funds. Like receiving dividends directly from shares, the fund, once it has declared a dividend, either has to pay it to you directly or buy additional units in the funds you have selected. I have *assumed* a net yield of 3.9 per cent. Because the dividend was paid to you as part of your ISA arrangement, you are not liable to tax.

The Pension

There are many ways to approach this matter, but in this example, I have said you will receive £5,000 tax free. With plans such as phased retirement pension income drawdowns, it's clear the industry has terminology most people find confusing. With crystallized funds, we are talking about the proportion of the fund you have accessed. To receive £5,000 from a pension pot of £100,000, we first have to crystallize £20,000 of the pot. From there, you can receive 25 per cent of £20,000 as a partial payment entitlement to your pension commencement lump sum (tax-free cash). This is why you pay no tax. This is distinct from someone who takes the full amount stated at the outset.

In a lot of cases, individuals take their tax-free entitlement and put it into a taxable environment by putting it in a building society. Thus, after you have received your £5,000, you are left with a cumulative fund of £95,000. Of the latter sum, you have:

- £15,000 invested in a crystallized fund
- £80,000 in a non-crystallized fund

Your £95,000 is still invested, and as a result, it is still exposed to investment risk. This means that, in the end, you could receive either more or less than if you taken the full 25 per cent from the outset. I could also write a few more pages about how this has changed the death benefits on this fund, but the purpose of this book is to describe efficient ways of receiving passive income. Again, if you're interested in these matters, I recommend getting independent financial advice.

You are also allowed to receive income from the potentially taxable element of your pensions (the remaining 75 per cent). Currently, you are entitled to income between 0 per cent and 120 per cent of a conventional annuity, a figure based on a formula dictated by the government's actuarial department. This is known as the GAD rate. The upper maximum limit is different in each case because it is based on (among other factors) your age, the size of your fund, and general mortality factors.

In this example, I have *not* opted to take income; I have simply used some of the tax-free entitlement as income. Currently, the access age range to receive benefits from these types of pensions is between ages 55 and 75.

You can see that, by using different asset classes, you can benefit from asset class diversification and receive tax efficient passive income. The main risks to this approach are inflation and investment. Inflation is a risk because your portfolio has to grow by 5 per cent *plus* the rate of inflation to put you back into your starting capital situation. Investment is a risk because your funds will rise or fall based upon where they are invested.

Idea 6: Using Premium Bonds as a small hedge.

I have included this item because, if you get a return, it is at least passive income and tax free—despite the fact that, in recent times, payouts have been reduced. If you get no return, the amount of your investment will be subject to inflation risk. In such a case, though your capital is guaranteed, it has been devalued.

Generally, premium bonds are used as a hedge or for risk-averse investors. I came across an interesting website recently: premiumbondcalculator.com. The site will give you an indication of likely returns. One example: if you had £1,000 in cash ISA that paid 3 per cent over the year, it would pay only £30. If you had the same amount in premium bonds, there was a 60.7 per cent chance you would receive less than that amount. If you invested the maximum (£30,000), you would receive £900 in cash ISA. There is a 96.1 per cent chance you would receive less than that amount if you invested in premium bonds.

The only real advantage I can see is, like cash ISAs, you have almost immediate access to your capital. Plus, there is no investment risk.

Idea 7: Info-preneuring and online marketing

Coming from an age and from a business background as I did that was laced and locked down with bits of paper, it is difficult to imagine a business world without paper. But those of us who have not embraced the digital world must do so or get left behind.

It is difficult for people of a certain age to imagine how we used to survive in business before the explosion of the Internet age. This is why so many things have become redundant. Consider the following things:

- public telephone boxes
- fax machines
- chequebooks
- handwritten letters
- receiving pay by a pay packet first, and then by cheque
- putting a sticker on your car that said, *tax disc in the post!*
- buying music on vinyl, tape, and CD

Earlier, items such as microwaves, blenders, freezers, power tools, TVs, video players, home recording equipment, and cameras were purchased just as they are today. But when these items broke, they were fixed because it was the cheapest option. Nowadays, it is often cheaper to throw the item away (or recycle it) and buy a replacement. If you buy a PlayStation console, for example, it will be out of date soon. Who still has an original PlayStation console? Own up, if you dare.

The problem with *stuff* is that we don't like to discard it a lot of the time. The result is that most of us have things lying around our houses that we should have thrown out or given to someone who needed it. Because, in the main, people do not do this, the items fill our homes, taking up space that will never be used again.

I offer this information because, in business, the equivalent is loving paper. In business, we have millions of bits of paper that are now useless, but we won't or can't shred them and get rid of them. I suspect that people stopped printing out every bit of non-spam e-mail quite recently. In the government and in the legal profession, the situation is dire. In my profession, we are usually required to have a bit of paper for everything from a now-your-customer fact find to contracts that require a wet signature to meaningless summary statements that are sent out by financial product providers every day.

The *true* info-preneurer cannot remember the last time he or she printed off anything, yet he or she has a thriving and profitable business. But what is info-preneuring? And why is it a source of true passive income?

The term is a merger of two words: *information* and *entrepreneur*. These days, you don't have to wait for a newspaper to turn up on your doormat to collect the news, it is *instantly* available. Often, social network sites, such as Facebook and Twitter, create the news rather than just report on it. In the past, the business owner had time to respond to customer queries by returning phone calls or writing letters. Now, he or she is required to respond *instantly* to emails, scanned documents, and Skype conference calls. Many big retail chains have fallen because they could not adapt quickly enough.

There are, of course, notable exceptions. One of the most profitable businesses on the planet—whether you love them or loathe them—is McDonald's. Many years ago, new trainee managers of McDonald's were asked by senior management to name the secret of the company's profitability. The silence in that particular classroom must have been deafening. Finally, one trainee manager who could not comprehend the stupidest question he had ever heard came back with the answer, 'Hamburgers, of course!' But he was wrong. The real brilliance of the balance sheet of McDonald's is real estate. You only have to look at your high street to notice that the place that used to house a huge pub or hotel in the High Street is now a McDonald's outlet.

This company thrives due to the franchise options it has, and it makes a fortune buying and leasing back to the new franchisee the outlet they will be working in. Simple and brilliant. They are one of the exceptions, one of the companies that should have a High Street presence. Food is a non-cyclical business because, whether our economy is riding high or deep in recession, whether we are happy or depressed, we all have to eat. And if you have the right brand, you are home and hosed.

Most info-preneurs realize they do not need to have the cost of a retail outlet. They realize they can set up a cost-efficient website and distribution process online. This could be selling products, selling information, or selling advertising. Some even have their own classes online. Many sell adverts by working with companies such as Google. Some have a website that is subscription based; some have blogs that you have to pay to follow. What is the beauty of this?

- very low cost, including the set-up cost
- no need for premises
- no need for storage space

- no need to buy and store stock
- no more paper, just text and image ads that are probably paid for by advertisers

Once you have got all of this set-up, there is little need to spend much time on it. For this reason, it qualifies as passive income.

Idea 8: Royalties

If you are creative and have a skill, you could be earning passive income. My daughter, Jo, is a great example. Even when she was a child, I knew she had a good voice: she could shout across the road in heavy and noisy traffic to alert her brothers to the fact that their dinner was ready. I was standing by her and thought my eardrums had burst. She has a fantastic voice *and* an incredible range. She can hit top notes I did not think existed.

She always loved music. Later on, she was signed to a girl band, Smoke 2 Seven, which went on to have a couple of minor hits. Jo realized early on that the true wealth in music was in its passive income potential. That is, the money was in writing the songs, producing them, and managing the musicians. The music industry seems very fickle to me. On the negative side, you have only a small chance of signing the next Rolling Stones, but on the positive side, you probably only need one major hit to make it., Jo created a girl band named Stooshie. She has more bands in the pipeline and is going places. She has worked very hard to get where she is. All of her previous activity was linear, but now she is at the point that the balance is swinging **sharply** towards passive income.

If you write a song that is even moderately successful, you get paid *every time* it is played. In the supermarket near my house in Spain, I kept hearing a song that Jo wrote every time I was in there shopping. When Jo told me how much she got paid every time it aired, I gave her my shopping bills!

If music is not your skill, what is? I like writing; hence, this book. I have no idea how much it will earn, but I am enjoying the writing process. And if only a small percentage of you buy this, I will have succeeded. We cannot all be JK Rowlings, but if getting royalties is only one of your passive income streams, you are likely to benefit from a diverse portfolio.

In the case of writing, once you have written your piece—it could be a book, blog, or magazine article—you can sell it online, find a publisher willing to take a risk, or pay for the cost of publishing yourself.

Idea 9: Franchising

Like most other asset classes, franchising starts life as linear activity, but if approached correctly, it should become passive. Here are a few companies with loads of potential:

Telecom Plus

This company is listed as The Utility Warehouse. Started in the nineties, this is a listed company that offers gas, electricity, fixed-line telephone services, and Internet services. At the time of this writing, the company boasted over 430,000 customers in the United Kingdom.

The company's services are sold by self-employed distributors. Why is this passive income? Simply, the rep selling the service gets a percentage of the bill every time the customer introduced by the rep picks up the phone, goes on the Internet, or puts on the central heating to get warm. Furthermore, every time an existing rep introduces a new rep, he or she gets a percentage of that person's income.

The company holds an interesting position. In 2012 and increasingly so in 2013, a lot of criticism was levied at the biggest utility suppliers due to the size of their profits. This provides The Utility Warehouse with a good competitive edge.

Yes, you will probably have to work hard initially to get this off the ground, but the whole concept is designed to create income that will be passive. The Utility Warehouse has far lower costs than the majors, and I believe it will expand.

Other Franchises

Because I have mentioned The Utility Warehouse that trades as Telecom Plus, I should mention *franchises* generally. They qualify under my list as long as, at some point, you have staff running them for you. You should sell your stake or stop when you are receiving enough income. You are advised to work *on* your business instead of *in* it.

At the beginning, you will need to pay the cost of the franchise, and then you will need to work hard to get the business up and running . . . not only with turnover, but also with at least one year's growth and profit. Only then can you start thinking about subletting it. If you Google *franchises,* you will see lots of them on the Internet, one of them may suit your background and/or experience.

I also like the look of Moneysave. Among other services, they offer debt management counselling and customer-creditor negotiation for a fee. As a distributor, you will receive an income of that fee, and because you have paid a franchise fee, you are likely to receive leads based on your location.

I like the look of this company not just because of my background, but because I believe we are heading for a debt explosion. As people's net disposable income continues to drop due to more and more redundancies, more and more increased costs, and more and more part-time employment offers, the masses will slip into the debt mire. A lot of it may be self-inflicted, but a healthy proportion of it will be new, innocent parties.

dy wants something. How something's value is perceived is dependent upon many factors, including market sentiment, supply, and demand.

Gold

Gold has always held its value, and it is the commodity that people have always turned to when economic times are hard. It has proven to be an inflation buster. At the time of this writing, the price of an ounce of gold has risen by over 118 per cent over the past five years. It costs over £1,000 per ounce.

It is considered a valuable store of value, and it is traded all over the world. It is a decreasing commodity. How many gold rushes do you hear about today? Of course, gold deposits will still be found, but over time, both people's trust in gold and its decreasing availability will push up its value further. Furthermore, you only have to consider the growth of the world population over the last couple of decades to see that we will have a decreasing supply coupled with an exponential increase in demand. Supply and demand: the crucial factors that dictate the value of an asset.

There are many ways to buy gold: coins, bars, bullions, and gold funds. The most commonly traded gold coins in the United Kingdom have been South African Krugerrands and British Sovereigns, historically. They can be bought easily enough online through sites such as ebay.com. Alternatively, you can go directly to an online supplier.

You can buy gold physically, too. One of the best-known UK destinations I favour is the jewellery quarter in the centre of Birmingham. I received better deals there than anywhere in London. Another location for selling is in Southall. The town has numerous jewellery shops that will offer you a good deal. But do your research when you buy and sell items. You are looking for a profit that will roll into instant cash for income or investing.

The main disadvantages with buying physical gold are as follows:

- Someone could break into your house/storeroom/ secure area and steal the gold. Insurance to cover this kind of theft is likely to be expensive and would not be covered under any normal home contents policy.
- Where are you going to keep the gold?
- You cannot sell *part* of a bullion bar or gold coin (as you can, for example, with gold funds).
- You will need to wait a sensible amount of time after the purchase of the asset before you dispose of it for a profit. One way to gauge the value easily is to see what people are paying for the same item on the ebay.com.

Incidentally, you may have noticed that I have not listed ebay.com as a source of passive income. That is because, even if you make good profits on the site, you are still engaged full-time in linear activity. This only changes if someone else runs the operation for you (and after the costs of their wages are deducted, you are still making a profit).

Gold funds

You can buy gold funds via unit trust portfolios and/or exchange traded funds. (ETFs). The ETFs buy the physical gold, keep it in storage (thus removing your security and insurance risks). They then issue shares based on your holdings. An ETF trades in a similar way to a direct share, and it can therefore be bought or sold during the course of a trading day. If you are new to these products, it would make sense to get independent financial advice from a company that specializes in this type of advice. Have a good look around and check with at least three different providers. *Never* be taken in by persistent sales calls.

Similarly, you can buy other commodities, such as silver and platinum. Buying any commodity is likely to benefit as an inflation hedge, and over time, commodities benefit from demand. Often, however, you will need to be patient to receive a return.

Lead and plastic soldiers

When I was growing up, I was lucky enough to share a hobby with my father and another friend. Every other Sunday, we would take turns hosting a series of war games, following the rules of a well-known author, HG Wells and his game, Little Wars.

We enjoyed playing war games for many years, but unlike other war games, we had toy cannons and actually fired them at each other's soldiers. In retrospect, that was a silly thing to do. After all, like a lot of collectables, they had value that we were damaging. But at least we were having fun!

These days, if you have a collection of Britain's lead and plastic figures, they are worth a lot of money, especially the lead ones. The retailer that sold them, like most others, no longer exists. Thus, if you have a collection, it could be a very valuable inflation buster.

A huge number of people have collected just about everything from Airfix models to toy cars to action men to *Star Wars* and *Star Trek* figures to Barbie dolls. There are at least four disadvantages associated with collectables:

- Again, where are you going to keep them? Unlike gold and silver coins, they are likely to take up a lot of space.
- As with most collectables, if you have a sizeable collection, they will not be covered under a conventional home contents policy. You will have the additional cost of insurance and a security issue.
- HMRC will have an interest in any profit you make from buying and selling stock. If you sell regularly, the best advice is to declare your profits.
- You will need to keep all items in top condition to get the best price. Fundamentally, this means keeping the item in its original box.

SUMMARY

Anyone can start on the road to being totally financially secure, even with little investment to start. With the right attitude, plan, and devotion, you will wake up with the knowledge that you do not have to go to work unless you *choose to.*

I have included items that will give you a very wide investment approach. You should remember that no investment or approach is devoid of risk. Even if all of your money is on deposit in the most secure bank in the world, there is still risk.

Diversification, daily application, and constant research is the key to your ultimate success. Even if you start small, you can still think and grow big. Start off with a goal of £1,000,000. At 5 per cent (plus growth on top of that to combat inflation), you will earn £50,000 gross per year. This, I think, will let you avoid the need to go busking on dark railway platforms!

I am not going to wish you luck because you do not need luck for a successful passive income stream. Instead, you need the knowledge and the drive to succeed.

Lightning Source UK Ltd.
Milton Keynes UK
UKOW05f0221230114

225046UK00001B/7/P